Bumpy Roads Have Soft Shoulders
Living with NF

Bumpy Roads Have Soft Shoulders
Living with NF

NICOLE PORLIER

Copyright © 2013 by Nicole Porlier.

Library of Congress Control Number: 2013901811
ISBN: Hardcover   978-1-4797-8789-0
               Softcover   978-1-4797-8788-3
               Ebook   978-1-4797-8790-6

All rights reserved. No part of this book may be reproduced or transmitted in any form or by any means, electronic or mechanical, including photocopying, recording, or by any information storage and retrieval system, without permission in writing from the copyright owner.

This book was printed in the United States of America.

Rev. date: 4/19/2013

To order additional copies of this book, contact:
Xlibris Corporation
1-888-795-4274
www.Xlibris.com
Orders@Xlibris.com
128907

LIFE IS LIKE PHOTOGRAPHY,
YOU NEED NEGATIVES TO DEVELOP
— AUTHOR UNKNOWN

*Dear Mo and Jay,
Hope you enjoy my book and find it inspiring! Thank you for your support
Love Nicole*

To my parents, who gave me unconditional love and support.

To Daddy, I wish you were here. You left us far too soon, and I miss you dearly.

Maman, thank you for your strength and courage to help me persevere in all that I accomplished and all that I still wish to accomplish. I would not be the woman I am today without you. *Je t'aime.*

To my dear sisters, Nadine and Manon, who have provided me with unparalleled support when I needed it most. I have always looked up to you, and I am privileged to have such wonderful sisters. I love you both very much.

And to my dearest husband, Denis, I love you more than life itself. Thank you for accepting me for who I am, for helping me through my many difficulties with NF, for never giving up on me, and for loving me—bumps and all. You are my true love. I will forever love you and stand by your side.

TABLE OF CONTENTS

Introduction xi
What Is Neurofibromatosis? 1
My NF Diagnosis 3
School 5
My NF Experiences 13
Workshop Junkie 21
Picture Album 25
How I Met My Knight in Shining Armor 31
A Change of Heart and Attitude 37
My Life Today 41
My Trip to New York and Dr. Weinberg 43
My Path to Getting Fit 47
Secret to Happiness 51
Thank You 55
References 57
Index 59

INTRODUCTION

I believe in my own power to change
—Louise Hay

My name is Nicole Porlier, and I have neurofibromatosis, commonly known as NF. I wrote this book to give both children and adults who suffer from NF the hope and will to live happy, fulfilling lives despite the disorder's many debilitations. I understand it is sometimes difficult to keep a positive outlook on life, particularly in cases where NF negatively affects organs within the body, causing severe malfunctions and complications.

This is my story. My hope is that it may comfort you, encourage you, and inspire you to shine your inner light on the world.

WHAT IS NEUROFIBROMATOSIS?

Think it's hard to say? Imagine living with it.

NEUROFIBROMATOSIS IS PRONOUNCED *neuro· fibroma· tosis*, often referred to as NF.

Neurofibromatosis is an umbrella name for three distinct complex genetic disorders that share a common manifestation—tumor growth in the tissues that surround nerves within the body.

Most of these tumors are benign, although, occasionally, they can become malignant. NF can also cause additional complications, such as disfigurement, bone deformities, and learning disabilities. It is a disorder that equally affects males and females of all ethnic groups.

The three types of neurofibromatosis are the following:

- **Neurofibromatosis Type 1 (NF1).** This is the most common form, affecting approximately one in three thousand births.
- **Neurofibromatosis Type 2 (NF2).** This is a less common form, affecting approximately one in thirty-five thousand births.
- **Schwannomatosis.** Statistics show that this type occurs about as often as NF2.

NF1 is the most common form of neurofibromatosis, causing

developmental changes in the nervous system, skin, bones, and other tissues. Half of all cases of NF1 result from spontaneous genetic alteration, while the remainder are inherited from one or both parents.

NF1 affects each person differently. Some people are only mildly affected and may never come to know that they actually have the disorder, while others are more severely affected and require medical treatment. Each individual with NF1—even those in the same family—can be affected in a completely different manner.

Although twice as common as Duchenne muscular dystrophy, Huntington's disease, cystic fibrosis, and Tay-Sachs disease combined, NF is largely unknown and misunderstood by the general population. This lack of awareness results in an unfortunate sense of isolation in those living with NF. Even the medical community is largely unaware of this disorder, and there are evident difficulties in providing accurate and timely diagnoses. Even when general practitioners are able to detect the first symptoms of NF in a child, they are hesitant to make the diagnosis because they feel very little can be done—there is no cure, and treatment strategies are still in the trial stages.

MY NF DIAGNOSIS

Where hope grows, miracles blossom.

—Elna Rae

WHEN I WAS born, I had spots on my right leg and my neck. These spots are called café au lait, which translates to "coffee with milk." They look similar to a birthmark but are actually a symptom of NF1.

In my case, I have café au lait marks on my neck and also on my upper right leg. On various parts of my body, I also have freckles with spots inside them. These freckles, when they are a particular diameter apart from one another, can be a symptom of NF1. This same freckling pattern is also on my right leg.

I had no other signs or mental delays typical of NF1 to signify something was wrong. I was too young to understand, but the café au lait marks were the cause of some concern for my parents since the rest of my body was normal.

When my parents were told that I had NF, the doctor at the time also informed them that it was likely I would be a slower learner in school and would need to attend an institution for children with special needs.

Despite the doctor's prognosis, my parents, especially my mother, were confident they would do whatever it took to help me lead a normal life. They had full faith that we'd overcome this barrier. And we did.

SCHOOL

The difference between school and life? In school,
you're taught a lesson and then given a test. In life,
you're given a test that teaches you a lesson.
— Tom Bodett

IN SCHOOL, I faced challenges that made learning difficult and even frustrating at times. It took longer to understand the lessons, but once I put my mind to it, I discovered that I had the capacity to conquer anything.

My mother spent endless hours helping me study for tests. She would explain the material over and over again, giving me pointers on how to remember dates and important historical events. With clear examples and the sharing of her personal experiences and her parents', I was able to remember events more clearly, which bettered my chances of performing well on my tests.

Despite the anxiety, nausea, and excessive perspiration I experienced prior to any test, I overcame these physical distractions to do quite well throughout school.

My poorest subjects were math and science. Every time I was required to write a test for either of these classes, I would fail. These repeated failures affected my self-confidence and left me feeling depressed and unintelligent, without enough courage to continue.

Looking back on that now, I know my biggest fear was what people thought of me.

My parents never punished me for poor performance. They simply wanted me to prove that I was capable. They stressed that it was important that I always did my best and applied myself.

I did not enjoy school whatsoever. However, I attended one of the best private schools, called the Toronto French School. Raised by parents of European descent, my father from Switzerland and my mother from Belgium, I had the best of both worlds.

I attended the Toronto French School until grade 10 after which I decided to switch to a public school. The Toronto French School was too difficult, and there was far too much competition among students to attain the best marks.

As we all know, in high school, everyone desperately tries to fit in, which unfortunately often involves succumbing to various peer pressures to drink, smoke, do drugs, or have sex. I declined such offerings.

I had a few friends who shared my values and never pressured me to do anything I was uncomfortable with. Yet in terms of feeling a genuine sense of belonging, there was unfortunately no difference between my private and public school experiences.

When I entered North Toronto Collegiate in grade 11, I was fortunate enough to have a principal who understood my difficulties with math and science and allowed me to go through school without these subjects. I felt as though I was the luckiest student who'd ever lived. I completed my final year focusing on language classes in French, English, German, Spanish, and French literature. I had found an area of study in which I excelled and completely immersed myself in it. This changed my mind-set from inadequate to confident and capable. For some students, language was not their forte, but I loved it! I enjoyed talking and communicating in different languages because it made me feel like I came from several different cultures. For the person I was speaking with, I'm sure they were at least somewhat impressed that I was able to communicate in their native tongue.

In grade 11, students were approached by the counselor's office to entertain various career options. I was pegged to be a schoolteacher, and although it was a career I really wanted to pursue, I had to acknowledge my high school student struggles as well as the challenges I faced as a sufferer of NF. I decided to find a job where my linguistic abilities would be put to good use and one I was confident I would be able to perform well.

I took various German courses at the Goethe Institute in Toronto and studied German from grade 9 to 13. I studied Spanish from grade 11 to 13, and sometimes during March break, I traveled to Mexico to practice my Spanish with the local citizens.

The year I graduated, in 1985, I was given an opportunity to participate in an exchange program in Stuttgart, Germany, for three months. Unfortunately, the family I stayed with had a daughter who had very little interest in spending time with me. Thankfully, I met several other people and spent time with students who were a little younger than me. Since I spoke French fluently, I was able to help these students improve their French, and in turn, they helped me enhance my German-speaking skills. In the end, it turned out to be a highly enjoyable trip.

I also traveled to Tübingen, Germany, for one month, where I was enrolled in an intensive course of full-time classes in German. Funnily enough, it was actually my sister who was supposed to fill this spot, but she became unable to go. I was so eager to learn and had such a love for traveling, I jumped at the chance to travel yet again and engage myself in a terrific language course. It too was a memorable trip.

After high school, every job position I held was for bilingual reception or customer service roles.

In my twenties, I obtained a job at a hotel in Geneva, Switzerland. Here I was able to utilize French, English, and German.

Following this, I worked for a company by the name of Purchasing Management Association of Canada in Toronto but subsequently lost my job in 1996. I received severance pay, and my parents helped me through this tough time, encouraging me to do what I loved: travel and go to school. This was a phenomenal opportunity for me because eventually I would begin working again and would likely never have a chance such as this to take advantage of. I inquired about Spanish language schools and went to Cuernavaca, Mexico, for five weeks. I stayed with a family and requested they not speak a word of English to me and that I may be the only student in their home (in order to avoid the chance of English, French, or any other language being spoken with other students). This way, I had no choice but to speak the language. I used the dictionary often and many times over would ask, "How do you say this in Spanish?" This gave me an additional five to seven hours of grammar and conversation every single day, and I took advantage of all opportunities to speak the language. I submerged myself deep into the Mexican culture and loved every moment of it.

The fact that my parents began speaking French to me at a very early age made it much easier to be bilingual later in life. I have a strong passion to communicate in different languages. Over the years, I've realized that when you are passionate about something, you work hard to remove all obstacles in your path in order to succeed. I focused on my love for language rather than my challenges with NF.

I have had my share of pain living with NF; however, I am very grateful to have two extremely supportive parents and two wonderful sisters, who have all loved me unconditionally. I never felt as though I was a burden or a handicap to anyone in my family. I was able to do all the fun activities other kids do as they grow up, and my sisters often included me in their outings, even with their friends whom I always very much enjoyed.

Although I experienced the same tribulations most adolescents do in their teenage years—acne, glasses, puberty, social awkwardness—high school was very difficult for someone with NF. I was constantly told how ugly I was and how different I seemed compared to other students. I couldn't wait for school to be over.

During my teen years, I continued to develop symptoms of NF. This included the appearance of a couple of fibromas under my arm and one on my right bum cheek. I didn't have too many on my legs or my face at that time. I don't remember waking up one morning and seeing them in the mirror. The fibromas came gradually, and at that time, I really never understood what they were. My parents thought it would be a good idea to have the fibromas removed surgically, both for my own self-confidence and also to avoid the undoubtedly awkward questions from other children and their parents should I ever happen to swim in public.

Unfortunately, throughout my midteen years, my fibromas continued to appear. I started developing them on my hands, arms, stomach, breasts, and back. Of course not all areas were exposed, but in a girls' changeroom or whenever I wore a bathing suit, it was obvious I was different from other kids.

Twenty years ago, there was very little knowledge about NF; doctors knew very little, and very little research was conducted.

I had two of those fibromas removed—one under my arm and one on my right bum cheek, which came back shortly after the surgery as is typical with neurofibromas. I always believed it was the surgery that caused my fibromas to come back. I thought the doctor removed the stitches too soon, not giving the area enough time to heal properly. However, there is scientific evidence supporting the fact that fibromas can reappear after removal.

When the tumors are under the skin, they are known as dermal fibromas. It is unpredictable as to how many will emerge onto the skin and when. Typically, dermal fibromas surface as hormones increase during puberty. In addition, when these tumors are removed, they are removed superficially. NF tumors grow and wrap themselves around the nerves. Much like the dandelion that grows in your garden, if you just remove the head of the dandelion, you miss the root, thereby causing it to grow back. Only when you remove the core or the root can you be certain it will not grow back.

I know my teenage years were not easy for my parents. Like most teens, I fought for my independence and always wanted to be right. My mother and I sometimes argued because I thought she didn't understand me. Although she couldn't possibly know exactly what I was experiencing, deep down I knew she felt my pain every time I cried. She often cried with me, both of us expressing how unfair it was for me to live with NF.

When it came to my clothes and the way in which I dressed, my mom asked me to cover my arms, particularly areas where my skin bumps were most obvious. This bothered me. I wanted to be myself and, as a teenager, express myself through the clothes I wore. Yes, other kids stared at me, but my thoughts were simply, *Who cares?* I believed it was rude to stare at someone no matter who they were or what they looked like.

My mother's point of view was different. She thought, *Why expose yourself to hurtful stares and questions?* It was her way of protecting me. At my age, I wanted to have my own opinions and make my own choices. I have since learned that circumstances in life often beg the question, "Would you rather be right or be happy?"

I sometimes pretended to be strong and would say to my mom, "If someone wants to ask what I have, let them ask." Honestly, I am not sure how strong I would have been if someone had actually asked me in that moment.

In my teen years, I discovered a program called the Forum. The Forum is a three-day course that covers many different elements of life, including learning to let go and to forgive. The Forum helps people understand difficult situations. In the course, there were people in attendance who hadn't spoken to a family member in years, those who had experienced loss such as losing a job, and even those who blamed others for their present situations.

During my time as part of the Forum, I learned how to take responsibility for my actions. I took the course to restore my confidence and also to improve my relationship with my mother. During my healing journey, I realized that I blamed my mother for the fact that I had NF when, in reality, my mother's ultimate purpose in life was to protect me from the "bad wolves" in the world—both male and female. My mother's unconditional love helped me gain self-confidence and taught me to be a strong, independent woman with admirable values and the ability to love. At the time, however, all I could see was the fact that my mother wanted me to hide myself, which fundamentally opposed my personal views. Looking back, it was not as detrimental as I made it out to be. After all, I was hiding my arms, not my personality. And so often, I did feel as though people were staring and talking about me. It got to a point where I felt as though I came from a different planet, what with all the negative attention I received. My inner sadness and anger often showed through my facial expressions, making me appear as though I was constantly in a bad mood. I just had so much pain and anger in my heart that it was sometimes difficult to see my inner beauty since, on the outside, I looked terribly miserable. This misery, combined with the bumps on my skin, surely made me appear far less attractive than I really was.

MY NF EXPERIENCES

*Every experience I have leads me to a greater
understanding of my purpose on Earth.*

—Louise Hay

I HAVE HAD a variety of shocking and hurtful experiences as a result of NF. Looking back, I am still amazed at the insensitivity people have toward others who look different from themselves.

There was an incident quite a few years back in May of 1999. I remember it was a beautiful spring day. I had quit my job because I was very unhappy and decided to pursue a career as a travel agent. I was feeling excited since I had just enrolled in a six-month training program at the International Institute of Travel.

I decided to treat myself as a way to celebrate this new life path, and I walked into a nail salon located at the local mall. With an enthusiastic smile, I asked the lady working there if she was available for a manicure. Her response was horrific. She looked me up and down as though I'd come from a different planet, then immediately declined my manicure, telling me it was because of my skin condition. She said, "I can't give you a manicure because of your skin." I was in complete shock and walked out of the salon upset and angry. Then I stopped, turned around, went back inside, and asked to speak with the owner. I was brimming with anxiousness and anger.

It turned out that the woman who declined my manicure was, in fact, the owner. I informed her that I would be reporting her to the police for discrimination. I also told her how insensitive I thought she was. She told me to go ahead and report her. The police station, conveniently, was located directly across from the salon.

Still distraught and shaking all over, I made my way to the police station where I shared my story. The officer returned to the salon with me and asked the owner to apologize to me. Even after the apology, I was still upset, and I went a step further to report her business to mall management. I also called the Human Rights Commission and the local television station where I was given an offer to verbalize my complaint on a wider scale, but I declined. In the end, I wrote a letter to the owner and offered to meet with her to educate her about NF. Sadly, I received no response.

Over the years, I've realized that this was a valuable exercise for me because it taught me to stand up for myself, if for no other reason, for my own peace of mind. I felt good about what I did but was also very angry that I was forced to experience so much humiliation.

I decided not to take the salon owner to court because what it really boiled down to was the fact that I was simply declined a manicure. What I did do, however, was make sure her salon never received any recommendations from me.

I overcame this one particular incident but quickly learned that sometimes it isn't a stranger who offends you but someone you know. Years ago, I tried to follow up with a woman I'd met through a friend of mine. She seemed kind and friendly when I met her, and I was always very open to meeting new people, so we decided to have dinner together. When I suggested we meet again with some of her friends, thinking it would be fun to go out as a group, she told me I would not fit into her group of friends because

I was not pretty enough for them. This made me feel small and insecure. I am now thankful that I lost touch with her and never saw her again as she was certainly not a friend worth keeping.

I do, however, have my best friend, Clarissa, a woman I met while taking a computer course called Lotus 123 over twenty-five years ago. Do you remember the days of Lotus and Word Perfect? Clarissa and I have been friends ever since we took that course; it's hard to believe twenty-five years have gone by, and I can say with complete confidence that she is truly a diamond in the rough!

Not only have I gone through negative experiences in my personal life but also in my professional life. Years ago, I applied for a job as a bilingual receptionist through an employment agency. I dressed in a beautiful suit for the interview. In most cases, I managed to find my own jobs without the help of an agency, but in this case, I knew the owner and trusted I was in good hands. When I met with one of the employment counselors for a job I felt I was a good fit for, I was disappointed when the agent disallowed me to proceed further in the interview process. She said it was because I was not attractive enough and would therefore not be a good fit for the company. Fully bilingual, polite, dependable, willing to learn, and a team player, but still not good enough! She said I did not meet the "physique requirements" of the job! I reported her comments and actions to the owner of the employment agency because it was discriminating, not to mention unfair and unjust. Thankfully, the company recognized the injustice and fired the employment counselor immediately.

Given the fact that there was very little information about NF in the '80s, there were many misconceptions found on the Internet, including the false belief that NF was the "Elephant

Man's Disease," which it is not. Unfortunately, there were written communications on this comparison, and all those with NF were seen as ugly, deformed people who should hide in the shadows.

For me, the saddest part about living with NF is the fact that when people meet me, most never see beyond the fibromas. I try hard to look my best and stay positive, yet despite my efforts, many people only see the physical side of me.

When I was young, I would constantly ask my friends if they thought I was pretty. When the fibromas began to appear, I needed validation that I was still within society's definition of *attractive*. I am sure I made people uncomfortable with my constant need for approval, but I had such little confidence in my changing appearance, and it was important that I hear positive confirmation from others.

On a beautiful summer's day in 1990, I was subjected to what I consider to be one of my worst experiences. I was in France with a former friend named Iside, and we were sitting by a pool, enjoying the sunshine. I got up to dip my feet in the pool when a young boy came up to me and said that his mom wanted to talk to me.

I did not think anything of it when he asked. I thought perhaps his mother had overheard a conversation about our studies and had a few questions, but my goodness, I was in for a surprise! She was convinced she knew exactly what condition I had and that I was going to infect all the children in the pool because of it. I was beside myself! I asked her, "Tell me what you think it is that I have." Of course she did not say NF and mentioned something completely different. She then proceeded to call the person in charge of the pool. A lady approached me and, without giving me a fair chance to explain, asked me to leave and not to come back until I had a doctor's note proving I was not contagious.

These are just a few examples of the ignorance I have had to deal with throughout my life. This particular incident crushed me emotionally, and I reached a new low where I actually felt as though I wanted to end my life. I was extremely sad and depressed. I could no longer see a point in living. As awful as it would have been for those who love me, in that moment, all I could think of was the fact that I wanted to die—to end the awful pain I felt. As I look back, I understand this mother was merely concerned for her child's safety, but regardless, the pain still lingers.

Yet another experience, which also dramatically affected me, occurred when I was in my late twenties. My ex-boyfriend Bernard had come to the decision that we should part ways. He lived in France, and due to the far distance between us, our relationship just didn't seem to function properly anymore. Furthermore, Bernard had children of his own from a previous marriage, and it later became known to me that throughout the time we were together, he maintained a relationship with his ex-wife despite their separation. Bernard never had a problem with my NF; he accepted me for who I was, and we had a very wholesome relationship at the time. He often complimented me and wrote me many beautiful letters, always trying to help me understand and accept my NF.

The breakup experience was no different for me than it would have been for anyone else. A broken heart is a broken heart no matter who you are. After Bernard and I went our separate ways, I decided to take action in my love life and joined a dating service. There was a company located on the same floor as my work, and I thought this would be a good way to meet new people and possibly even a lifetime companion.

I took a leap of faith and spoke to one of the ladies at the dating agency. After giving her all my personal information, I described what I was looking for in a man, which included personality, hobbies, and specific character traits I valued.

I also told her I had NF but asked her not to write it down in my file and not to mention it to any of my prospective dates because I wanted them to see me for who I really was and not merely for my disorder.

Over the course of a few months, the dating agency connected me with several different men. The dates were odd since these men had absolutely nothing in common with me—not a single character trait or hobby I had identified as important. What I did notice, however, is that each of my dates had a physical disability. This didn't necessarily bother me, but since everything else appeared to be a mismatch, I found it quite strange.

I finally went to the agency's office and asked why none of the men I had been matched with had any of the characteristics I'd previously specified and why all the men had physical disabilities. The response of the agency was "No normal man could ever love you!"

I was in complete shock and could not believe someone had the nerve to say such cruel words to another human being. This experience destroyed any shred of self-confidence I had managed to build. I was ready to give up dating entirely. Once again, I felt very depressed. I began to think this lady's words were true. For the second time, I found myself wanting to end my life.

The thought of suicide came as a relief. With all the pain I was going through and the constant questions I had to face regarding my disorder, the thought of doing this for the rest of my life was unbearable. Just the same as my first unfortunate experience, I eventually overcame this one too, yet it left me feeling sad and vulnerable. I still think about it to this day and share the story with others who I know would never judge me but who would rather offer some sense of compassion and understanding.

Unpleasant interactions with those who were uneducated about NF continued to occur in my life.

In the spring of 2012, I went to a small salon for a pedicure and was enjoying the treatment when the aesthetician next to me turned and asked if I had ever considered surgery.

I asked her, "What for?" and her response was, "For your skin." I told her I didn't want to talk about my skin although I probably should have told her to mind her own business.

Similarly, in the fall of 2012, I decided I'd like to have a facial. I met the aesthetician briefly, and the facial went well. I was upset at the end of the treatment when I was advised that she wanted me to speak with the spa director. The aesthetician remarked that it was because everyone would see me and ask about my condition as I left the spa.

This of course was very offensive. She wanted to report me to the spa director for fear that someone else would see me! I think the aesthetician must have thought I was contagious although I clearly told her I was not. Or perhaps she was embarrassed to be seen with me as we walked out of the room. It is difficult to say exactly, but her actions were entirely uncalled for. She left the room to let me relax, but that only caused anxiousness and tears. When the aesthetician came to check up on me, I was already getting dressed, ready to go home. I was introduced to the spa owner. He was very friendly and asked me how everything was. To avoid becoming even more upset, I said everything was fine, but I did call later to complain. He was very professional and understood why I was upset, agreeing that the incident was completely unethical.

It seems as though almost every time I decide to do something to make myself feel better, it backfires and I feel worse. Most people get spa treatments to relax, unwind, and enjoy a little pampering. I left the salon feeling upset, humiliated, and discriminated.

Sometimes I feel as though it will never end. Living with NF, I've come to terms with the fact that I will face these cruel incidences for the rest of my life.

Both my mother and Denis advised me to stay away from spas and salons because these places are based on beauty, materialism, and a superficial sense of self. Most of the aestheticians I have met don't see beyond a person's physical characteristics. By performing treatments people enjoy, an aesthetician's job should make customers feel *better*, but many times, they simply try to upsell their products. Through direct experience, I know that when I visit a spa, I'm exposing myself to insults and questions. I do, however, like to take care of myself, and I'm determined to fight for my rights. Although I often feel emotionally hurt after my visits, I also feel strong for going. I constantly hope for a new result, but this almost never happens. I think to myself, I have a right to visit a spa the same way anyone else does, but I've come to realize the pain is just not worth it. I am better off giving myself a facial or relaxing in the comfort of my home with a glass of wine. How many spas offer *that*?

WORKSHOP JUNKIE

Healing is a matter of time, but it is sometimes also a matter of opportunity.
—Hippocrates (460 BC–370 BC)

ON MY PATH to healing, I went through a phase where I became a seminar junkie.

I wanted desperately to feel at peace with myself. I started attending all kinds of seminars, especially those on life improvement, enhanced self-confidence, and self-healing.

Whenever I would hear about an upcoming healing workshop, I'd beam with excitement. I thought *healing* literally meant the reversal of a disease. One healing therapy I experienced was called rebirthing. This form of healing involves a process where the practitioner takes you back to your mother's womb and you visualize a new birth. It was thrilling.

I know it sounds crazy, but I actually thought I could be reborn without the symptoms of NF or, if results were not quite this extreme, that I could at least learn to let go of the past. The concept invited seminar attendants to create a new birthday so we could start a fresh, new life, free of our negative experiences. To be honest, this was probably one of the wildest therapies I chose. I was vulnerable and a little desperate as I actively sought a cure. Rebirthing may have other definitions, but my personal interpretation was that I could be reborn without NF.

I was on a mission, and I tried almost everything, but of course, most single therapy sessions did not help in a way I hoped they would.

I tried to let go of my inner anger. I had a lot of resentment inside me, and I thought that if I could only let this go, I'd be better able to accept my NF and possibly even reverse the condition. Part of letting go involved reliving awful experiences to the point where I could actually feel old pain in the present moment. The instructor would then tell me to take a deep breath in, and as I breathed out, the idea was that I'd be able to let go of that experience. Once it is let go, it is replaced with positive energy, which is sometimes called white light.

During this time in my life, I read quite a few books. One author I came to love and respect was Louise L. Hay. I read each and every one of her books and practiced many of her meditations. She writes about letting go of emotions and believes it is important to release all anger and resentment and to embrace forgiveness. Just as important as it is to forgive others who have hurt you, you must forgive yourself for whatever personal blame you hold. Her books enabled me to understand that we create every thought we think, and if we can change our thoughts, we can change our lives. She refers to one's inner child, and this inner child is actually who we are as small children. We must embrace, acknowledge, and love ourselves unconditionally. We need to heal our childhood wounds in order to find peace as adults. If we love ourselves, we have much more love to give others, and with that, our love has the ability to resonate and multiply.

After reading her books, I began listening to some of her CDs, practicing her meditations, and reciting positive affirmations to myself.

Although I was unable to cure myself of NF, the journey I took as I followed Louise Hay's recipe for positivity brought me hope, faith, and a renewed outlook on life.

PICTURE ALBUM

North Toronto Collegiate Institute

The Toronto French School

BUMPY ROADS HAVE SOFT SHOULDERS

Top: my beautiful, wonderful supportive sisters, Manon and Nadine
Bottom: My beautiful family (right to left)
Nadine, Manon, Daddy, Mommy, and Nicole

Our house in Port Credit

Our babies, two brothers, Marshall and Guinness (from different fathers)! ☺

Myself and my best friend, Clarissa, in Times Square, New York City.

Our wedding day: September 5, 1998

Nicole and Denis, tenth-year anniversary in 2008

Author, Nicole Porlier

HOW I MET MY KNIGHT IN SHINING ARMOR

You've gotta dance like there's nobody watching,
Love like you'll never be hurt,
Sing like there's nobody listening,
And live like it's heaven on earth.
—William W. Purkey

ONE OF MY favorite songs that always makes me want to sing and dance along is called "It's Raining Men," written originally by Paul Jabara and Paul Shaffer. Strangely enough, it was pouring rain the night Denis and I met.

In this song, it says, "God bless Mother Nature, she's a single woman too, she took on the heavens, and she did what she had to do, she took every angel and rearranged the sky so that each and every woman could find the perfect guy!" I did, and this is my story.

In my late twenties, I attended a three-month life-altering course. The purpose of the course was to either reconnect with someone you had lost touch with, find the perfect job, or find your life partner.

My goal was to find my soul mate. Throughout the course, I discovered different ways to meet other singles. I joined a nature-lover singles group and also a singles social group that offered a calendar of various events to choose from where I could spend time with other single individuals.

In order to define my ideal soul mate, I made a list of qualities I was looking for in a man. I typed out, in capital letters, a list of twenty qualities. At the top of the page, it read, "My dream man is . . ." A few of my most important qualities were that he loved his family, was especially good to his parents, and treated people with respect. My soul mate would love animals, especially cats and dogs; have a job; and be a hard worker. The only physical trait I specified was that he be taller than me. I stuck my page of soul mate qualities on the fridge and read it every day for the duration of the course.

I joined the Single Gourmet for two years so that I could take my time getting to know different men by dating slowly and developing relationships. The Single Gourmet was not a dating agency but a membership-based singles organization where we had a calendar of events for the month and could freely choose any event, whether it was a cocktail party, a show, a dinner, or even a cruise for singles.

My first social event was a dinner and dance at a Chinese restaurant in Toronto. It had a pleasant atmosphere, and I mingled with a few people. When it came time to sit down at our assigned tables and seats, I sat next to a man named Denis. The first thing I noticed was that his name was spelled in the French style on his name card. So my first question when we introduced ourselves was whether he pronounced his name De-knee or De-nis. That question caused a spark of excitement, and for the rest of the evening, we spoke in French and only to each other! This was June 29, 1996. At the end of the evening, we exchanged phone numbers and, just one week later, went out on our first date at a restaurant called Thai Magic—and evidently enough, this is where our own *magic* began!

We dated for one year, and the day after my birthday on October 3, 1997, Denis proposed. This was the kind of moment worth reliving. Every time I think about it, I tear up with joy, remembering how excited I was to know that I was going to spend the rest of my life with the man I loved and who loved me in return and accepted me for who I was, NF and all! We were in Niagara Falls, visiting a friend just outside of Buffalo, when Denis proposed. Denis and I had dinner at the Old Stone Inn. Afterward, we went for a short walk, and Denis began openly expressing his feelings for me, telling me he loved me and that he wanted to spend the rest of his life with me. As we headed toward a set of stairs, there was a lantern. I began walking up the stairs when Denis stopped me. He proceeded to hold my hand as he took out a small box. There in that moment, he proposed. It was the best moment of my life. I practically screamed and, of course, said yes—probably one hundred times. I will never get over that moment. I think my heart actually stopped, and it felt great.

Sadly, that same weekend, tragedy hit, and my father passed away on October 5. Thankfully, my father and Denis had met a couple of times, so I have the peace of mind knowing that my father was confident his daughter would be well taken care of.

When he was in the hospital, before he passed away, I announced the news of our engagement. I remember his last words to me were, "I am losing my daughter."

I replied, "You will never lose me."

That weekend was filled with so many mixed emotions. While

I experienced immense grief over the loss of my father, with whom I was so very close, I was also filled with happiness about my engagement to Denis. It felt so good to know that I would be sharing the rest of my life with him.

My father and I had a very intimate relationship, and we could always talk about anything and everything. I often had nightmares about losing him and dreaded the day he would die. He loved life and always had a positive attitude. More importantly, he loved all of us so very much—my mother, myself, and my sisters—and always did everything in his power to make us happy. He died of a heart attack at the young age of just sixty-six. There isn't a day that goes by that I don't think of him.

Every year on my father's birthday, Denis and I go to a nice restaurant and order a special bottle of wine to celebrate his life and to enjoy a meal that I remember was one of his favorites when he was alive.

My mother and father made such a great pair, sharing in their willingness to do just about anything for my sisters and me. My mother continually expresses her unconditional love for us. Like most mothers, at times she was more protective than I would have liked, but it was always for my own good. My mother is healthy but has also experienced a few issues along the way, especially over the past four years. There have been a few times where my mother was so unwell that we were scared we'd lose her too. When my mother is away in Florida, I visit her apartment to look after a few things on her behalf. The apartment feels so empty, and I often have awful thoughts of losing her, which scare me to my very core. I hope and pray she will live to be at least one hundred years old. This way, I'll be able to say that I've loved my mother for a full century (even though of course the love won't stop there). If it's true that we choose our parents at birth, then I must admit I have very good taste because I believe I have the best parents in the world.

As I matured, the relationship between my mother and me drastically improved. We attended seminars both separately and together in order to better our relationship and understand each other. As women, we each have a need to communicate and open up to each other. Over the years, I've also realized that it is impossible to change someone else and that you can only change yourself, how you think and how you act. In a single instant, you can change your thoughts or turn a bad mood into a good one. It all depends on how stuck or how miserable you want to be that day. I've learned you always have a choice. Although this concept sounds simple, it is not always easy to execute because sometimes you just need to be in a certain state (even if it's a negative one) until you are ready to change it.

As difficult and painful as some of the interactions have been throughout my life, many have made me stronger. After so many incidents, you learn to harden your heart for cruel people. I always remind myself that those people don't matter in my life and likely have their own problems to deal with. These people are not my friends and are unworthy of my time and friendship.

There are, however, a few experiences that changed my life forever. The one I'm about to tell had an impact on my life greater than any other. At the time, I'd been through so many unpleasant experiences. I was so fed up and didn't know how I could possibly handle any more. This particular incident, in and of itself, was not all that horrific, but unfortunately, I was at the end of my rope.

It occurred while I was waiting at a pharmacy to ask a question about a product. When it was my turn to talk with the pharmacist, I realized that an older man was listening in on our conversation. Suddenly, he chimed in entirely uninvited. Instinctively, I knew right away what I was in for. I was at the pharmacy inquiring about a possible solution for foot cramps and this nosy stranger interrupted us to ask about my skin!

Although this type of incident was fairly insignificant in comparison to other more hurtful situations, the old man, quite indirectly, actually helped me. At that moment, I was unwilling to explain myself to a complete stranger, and I'd hit my limit of dealing with curious, nosy, uninformed people. Since then I've realized that the best solution is to tell people what my skin condition is so that those who are uninformed may become informed.

But first, when I left the pharmacy on this particular day, I went home and unleashed a fury of tears. I told Denis that I never wanted to go out again unless I wore a bag over my head. I refused to be seen in public as the object of people's rude stares and uncontrollable curiosity.

A CHANGE OF HEART AND ATTITUDE

*The only person who can pull me down is myself, and
I'm not going to let myself pull me down anymore.*
—C. Joy Bell

I EVENTUALLY STOPPED crying, and from that moment on, I decided I was no longer going to let people hurt me. It was time to take control of my life and not feel sorry for myself or let others feel sorry for me either.

I took the next day off work and got in touch with the national NF organization, NF Canada, as well as the BC Neurofibromatosis Foundation and the NF Society of Ontario. I was eager to get involved, to help others living with the disorder, to promote awareness, and to raise funds for research.

One of the ways I worked toward these goals was through the use of business cards I created myself. On one side, there was information about NF and on the other, links to related websites.

When I created the cards, I chose a landscape with a mountainous background. The idea behind the image was that I could climb any mountain and overcome however many more obstacles came my way with a positive attitude. I handed out these cards just the same way you would a regular business card. People walked away with information about NF and with the option to learn more about it. I thought this was a great way to start spreading awareness about a condition that is common but not well known.

One of the first opportunities I had to hand out my card was while I was waiting for the train headed to Toronto at the Port Credit GO station in Mississauga. A lady approached me and asked me if I was contagious. I looked at her and smiled and said, "Actually I am!" Of course, she was surprised. I continued the conversation by asking her if she was serious about her question. Did she really think I would be in a public place if I were contagious? I gave her my card. This same woman told me that she'd previously approached a Jamaican man with dreadlocks to ask for drugs. The man asked if her assumption was based on the fact that he was Jamaican with dreadlocks, and she replied, "Yes!" This demonstrates how prevalent stereotypes are in our society and how people so easily jump to conclusions when they don't have enough information or refuse to take the time to get to know a person who looks different than they do.

Following this, I took the next logical step and joined the board of directors of NF Canada. I participated for about one year. During my time there, I helped organize an auction that raised money that was used to send teens diagnosed with the disorder to a unique NF camp in Utah. It took quite a bit of time and effort to elicit items for the auction. My auction partner, Natasha, and I collected over a hundred items to present at the auction. We didn't reach our goal to send one child to the NF camp; we had raised enough funds to send *three*!

I have made the choice to let people's comments and stares simply roll off my shoulders. This decision completely changed my attitude and in turn, my life. I'm a product of positive living in every way.

Strangely enough, when I reflect on my life, I really don't

consider it a bad journey. When I think of how many disasters, shootings, and diseases take people's lives far too soon, I know I have much to be grateful for.

I know this now, but as a younger woman, I was always offended when I was told that I was lucky to walk, talk, hear, and see. As a teenager, all I could see was the fact that my life with NF wasn't the life I wanted. Only now as an adult do I give thanks for my life and recognize the abundance I have.

Sometimes we struggle to see what we have to be thankful for. In one of the meditations I learned from Louise Hay, it tells you to give thanks for your bed where you can rest easily and be thankful for the source of electricity you have, the abundance of water you have access to, and all the means of transportation that are available.

Louise Hay taught me to look at everything in a much different way than I did before. The experiences that have caused me so much pain have also taught me so much about myself and have ultimately helped me become stronger and more accepting of all the effects of NF.

MY LIFE TODAY

There are three words I like to repeat to myself, glass half full, just to remind myself to be grateful for everything I have.

—Goldie Hawn

I AM NOW forty-six years old. I live in a beautiful house in Port Credit, Ontario, with Denis. We adopted a dog named Marshall from the Oakville & Milton Humane Society, and he is the most wonderful pet. We also have a cat named Guinness, also adopted from the Oakville & Milton Humane Society. Guinness is perfect for me as he is very affectionate and is all about the kisses! I almost changed his name to Kisses! I was connected to the Humane Society because I actually volunteered there for about a year and a half. I was a cat socializer, which meant that, one at a time, I would take each cat out of its cage for ten to fifteen minutes for playtime and human interaction. I volunteered a couple of hours a week and was able to meet so many wonderful animals, many of which found their permanent homes through the Humane Society. Adopting Marshall and Guinness made me so happy as they too found a happy home with us.

About ten years ago, I went through a couple of surgeries to remove fibromas that really bothered me. The surgeon, however, was not able to remove the fibromas on my chest because there are so many close together, making them very difficult to remove. Unfortunately, I also had fibromas on my breasts. This is a very sensitive subject because I felt as though my femininity was taken away from me when I had my nipples removed due to large fibromas surrounding the area. It took me a while to overcome this, but I managed to find solutions from women who had a similar experience when their breasts were removed due to cancer. I discovered they sometimes wear special bras. At least this made me feel a little better, and I did the best I could with what I had.

Over the past couple of years, I have met many more people with NF. I met one lady through Facebook. Her name is Marla, and we have since become good friends. We went out for dinner one evening with Marla and her husband, Tom, and spent the evening exchanging stories when she mentioned a doctor in New York who specialized in NF and who had a special procedure to remove fibromas. I was so excited I could hardly wait to tell my mother.

MY TRIP TO NEW YORK AND DR. WEINBERG

New York, New York
"I'm in a New York state of mind!"

AFTER SPEAKING WITH Marla, I immediately sent the information over to my mother and my sisters as well as my uncle George in Belgium.

I went to Dr. Weinberg's website to gather more information about his procedure and began preparing questions to ask at the appointment. As soon as I saw results from other patients on his website, my intention was to fly to New York immediately for the surgery.

This procedure is called electrodessication. It is a procedure performed by laser, which allows for the removal of five hundred to one thousand fibromas or small tumors in a two-hour period. Depending on the severity of the NF, it can take longer to remove certain fibromas, and the bigger tumors are removed by modern surgical technologies.

I called the secretary, Shamika, and asked to speak with Dr. Weinberg. I also arranged for him to speak with my mother so that she could have peace of mind about the surgery. I asked for references from other patients with NF who had gone through the procedure.

The next step was to book the surgery and my flight to New

York. This was in June of 2011. My mother came with me, which was such a relief for both of us because we knew we had each other, not to mention the fact that my mother had witnessed my pain so many times as I went through my challenges and heartaches with NF, and it was so important for her to be there with me.

We arrived safely in New York and took the subway to our hotel. The New York subway was a new and fun experience for us in the city. I admire my mother for her courage and willingness to take this route, since it was of course a longer journey.

We had an appointment to meet with Dr. Weinberg to discuss which fibromas I wanted him to concentrate on removing. I asked him to focus on my face, mostly in the chin area, my neck, and a few spots on my arms.

That evening, my mother and I relaxed, feeling quite tired from our day of travel. We stayed at a nice hotel, which had a beautiful rooftop patio overlooking New York City. We enjoyed a few drinks, and I slept very well that night. I was excited about the surgery and the hope of a future without fibromas.

The morning of the procedure, I was very nervous—in tears, in fact—fearing that the procedure would go terribly and that I might not even come out of it. I almost changed my mind, but since I had traveled all the way to New York, I knew there was no turning back now. I simply had to trust that it would be successful. Since I was asleep during the procedure, the hardest part was the waiting time for my mother. Thankfully, she was close to shopping areas and did her best to keep herself distracted—although I'm sure I was on her mind the entire time.

Once I arrived at the clinic, I was in good hands and treated very well. It was a private clinic, so the nurses were constantly by my side.

When the anesthesiologist arrived, he explained the dosage of the anesthetic and said he would be my personal bartender. I immediately requested a cosmopolitan martini. He laughed and said I could have as many martinis as I wished, and after that, I passed out. Those cosmos must have been strong!

I woke up later, safe and sound, and the procedure was a success. Dr. Weinberg explained that the fibromas that had been removed would be red and would eventually form scabs similar to chicken pox. The scabs would fall off within a few days or longer, depending on the area.

I was instructed to put a special cream on the areas to ensure proper healing. I took antibiotics to avoid infection and was given a different cream to control the itchiness of the scabs. The itchiness was quite intense, but it was also a sign of healing. It was very uncomfortable at first and felt as though I had mosquitoes buzzing nonstop around my face, and I desperately wanted to chase them away!

The following year, in February of 2012, I returned to New York for a second surgery, but this time with my best friend, Clarissa. During that time, my mother was not well and, therefore, was unable to travel, but she knew Clarissa well and was confident she'd take good care of me. Before my surgery, Clarissa took me everywhere to explore New York City. We had so much fun. The day of the surgery, she brought me food, flowers to brighten my day, and bandages for the areas that were red. I slept for the rest of the day.

The next day, we didn't waste any time. We were up and about bright and early, discovering more sights.

Since the first surgery was successful, Dr. Weinberg removed even more fibromas during my second surgery, including those on my stomach, as well as a few more on my face and neck.

I am very fortunate to have had these surgeries. They weren't cheap, and I had no medical coverage at the time (although such procedures would not have been covered by a medical insurance plan anyway since they took place in the United States). My mother felt they were well worth the money if they made me feel better about myself. I definitely did feel better as I had fewer bumps on my face, neck, and stomach. This procedure was not a cure by any means, but I did have fewer fibromas afterward, and overall, this gave me more confidence.

MY PATH TO GETTING FIT

Strength does not come from physical capacity.
It comes from an indomitable will.
—Mahatma Gandhi

WHEN I MOVED to Port Credit, I was very much looking forward to taking long and enjoyable walks along the lake since we now lived so close to the water. There were even a few designated waterfront trails, and these were especially beautiful.

Since I was on a new mission to get fit, I inquired about walking clinics at the Running Room store in our neighborhood.

The Running Room had early walks on Sunday mornings and evening walks during the week. At first, I objected as I never thought I'd be motivated to wake up extra early on a Sunday or give up my precious evenings with Denis. I also wasn't sure I'd be able to leave our store early to take regular daily walks (which would be necessary if I wanted to keep up with the training).

After I carefully analyzed these personal objections of mine, I decided it was time to put my health first. I joined the clinic in the spring of 2011.

Each week, our clinic walks became longer and longer. On Sundays, our clinic would walk up to ten kilometers and sometimes more, depending on the group. I enjoyed these walks for both the camaraderie and the beautiful scenery as we walked around Port Credit.

Many people at the Running Room train to do either a full or half marathon. The most popular were the Mississauga Marathon in May and the Scotiabank Toronto Waterfront Marathon in October.

I decided to keep walking and joined the half-marathon training that June. I almost never missed a week! Prior to completing the Scotiabank Half Marathon (twenty-one kilometers), I walked the fifteen-kilometer walk called Midsummer Night's Run. I found this one really tough, but I still finished! It felt amazing to receive a medal as I crossed the finish line and saw Denis there cheering me on.

I continued the walks and decided not only to walk the half marathon but also to participate in a walk to raise funds for NF. For the Scotiabank Waterfront event, anyone participating could raise funds for a charity of their choice.

I had my NF hat and shirt, and on October 16, 2011, I crossed the finish line after walking my twenty-one kilometers and raised $1,200.

It was such a wonderful feeling, crossing that finish line knowing I'd raised money for such an important cause.

June 2012 was my fourth clinic with the Running Room. We trained for the Scotiabank Waterfront event again, but this year, I walked with Denis and other friends from different cities. This was another tremendous accomplishment, this time walking as a group for NF.

We raised almost $8,000 and were so thrilled to know that these funds went toward research for an NF cure.

That fall, it took me longer than usual to bounce back from the marathon. I was feeling tired as I had trained hard for the event and had also begun personal training sessions with a woman named Jill. These sessions made me stronger and gave me better endurance to finish the race. I had been training with Jill since April 2012 and had never seen such incredible results—I lost body fat, gained muscle, and was more toned than ever before. My regular walks combined with these workout sessions have given me strength and greater self-confidence.

In the fall of 2012, I was given an opportunity to teach one of the clinics at the Running Room. Enthusiastic about the walks and knowing this would be the perfect way to stay fit and practice my leadership skills at the same time, I immediately accepted.

Along with my walks three times a week, I continue to train with Jill as well as on my own to continually maintain a healthy body and a sharp mind. In the spring, I plan to take up rowing and possibly join a dragon boat team. This will be another great form of exercise to tone my shoulders and give me more upper-body strength. I am not aiming to be a bodybuilder of course, but I like to have variety. As they say, variety is the spice of life!

SECRET TO HAPPINESS

Happiness comes of the capacity to feel deeply, to enjoy simply, to think freely, to risk life, to be needed.
—Storm Jameson

THE SECRET TO happiness is . . . there's no real secret. Just like secrets to success or to losing weight, the real secret lies in one's heart.

As I wrote this book, I realized more and more that, despite NF, I have accomplished a great deal in my life and I still have a long life ahead of me.

There is an abundance of books on the perfect diet, how to lose ten pounds in ten days, seven secrets to success, or the top twenty-five tips on how to market one's business. In reality, although these resources may be somewhat useful, only once a person starts to feel genuinely satisfied with their life does everything really fall into place. When we look for something else outside of ourselves for satisfaction—the perfect partner, a better job, a nicer home, a faster car—we're never satisfied.

I now realize that, as much as life has been tough at times, my experiences have taught me a great deal. I can now move forward knowing that it *is* possible to live simply and find peace and satisfaction in one's heart. Happiness can be found by opening your heart to others or by performing random acts of kindness to make this world a better place. And it can all be done despite people's curiosity or ignorance, despite the roadblocks that stand in your path, and despite the downfalls, trials, or tribulations no matter how large.

For me, it has now become apparent that in the end, when people ask what my skin condition is, it is actually a positive circumstance because my answer can only improve their education and appease their curiosity. Before long, a ripple effect will occur as I spread the word around the world about neurofibromatosis and many other lesser-known diseases.

I remember speaking at the Neurofibromatosis Society of Ontario Annual General Meeting (AGM) for the first time in October of 2011. I don't often speak in front of groups and was nervous at the time, but I was there to speak about my surgical experience.

I remember slouching a little in my chair as the person before me spoke. She was an engaging, confident speaker. All of a sudden, I sat up straight, rolled my shoulders back and decided to adopt the same confidence she had. I brought it on stage with me. My presentation went well, and I spoke quite clearly and positively. I was even approached by several people afterward who wanted to ask me questions and also received follow-up e-mails when the day was over.

The success of my presentation felt great compared to all those times throughout my life where I, more often than not, felt self-conscious about my appearance. I tried to look my best, but it was inevitable that, sometimes, I'd surely be looked at in a peculiar way.

My best advice for those with NF who feel down and lonely is to love and accept yourself just the way you are.

When you change your outlook on life and put a big smile on your face, it takes you farther than you could ever have imagined, and nobody will be able to pull you down.

As a matter of fact, this advice applies to anyone, not only those affected by NF. A smile on someone's face has the ability to seduce the world. This is something my mother wrote in a birthday card to me one year, and it made me feel so special. I've kept those words close to my heart ever since, and now I can truly say that each time I smile, I feel as though I really am enchanting the world. I can finally be seen as a special person for who I really am and not only as someone who suffers from NF.

My glass is always half-full and ready to be filled with more love and greater accomplishments.

May your glass always be at least half-full too!

THANK YOU

THANK YOU TO all my dear friends for your continued love and support. I'm so grateful for all the times you listened to me speak about my challenges with NF. You've always been wonderful friends, and I could never have reached this point without you. I love you all so much.

A very special thank you to my best friend, Clarissa, for always being there for me over the last twenty-five years and many more years ahead, I'm sure. I know sometimes I took you down with me through my NF struggles and pain, and for this, I will forever be sorry, but please know how much I appreciate your love, support, and unconditional friendship over all these years.

To Angela, who one day over breakfast told me, "You know, Nicole, you should write a book about NF!" Thank you, Angela, for helping me achieve this life-altering goal. I did it!

Muchas gracias to my Spanish teacher, César, for helping me improve my Spanish. I hope to have my book translated into Spanish someday.

Thank you to my friend and life coach, Desiree. You have taught me to always reach for the stars. Thank you for your help with my book in its beginning stages, giving me great ideas to make it fun and interesting to read. For this I am truly grateful.

Thank you to my more "secondary" life coaches, Anthony Robbins and Ley-Ann, for helping me through some difficult life obstacles.

Thank you to Wendy Brookes. Wendy, you have made me feel stronger especially on a spiritual level. For the first time I can truly say that I am in love with life.

To my personal trainer and friend, Jill. You've supported me and helped me reach my goals to be healthy, fit, and strong. With your help, I was able to restore my self-confidence, allowing me to love my body and myself for who I am.

To all my customers who helped me raise money for NF and, with those funds, get one step closer to finding a cure for children of the future, I cannot thank you enough.

REFERENCES

Nadine Marshall
Author's sister
Artist of the front cover of the book, "Path to Light"
www.nadineswork.com

Jill Pasma
Fit Bunnies Fitness
www.fitbunnies.ca

NFSO
Neurofibromatosis Society of Ontario
www.nfon.ca

Katie McDonald
Toronto copywriter
www.strikingcontent.com

Dr. Hubert Weinberg
http://www.hweinbergplasticsurgery.com/neurofibromatosis.php

INDEX

A

aesthetician, 19–20
agency, employment, 15

B

BC Neurofibromatosis Foundation, 37
birthday, father's, 34

C

children, 3, 9, 16–17, 22
Clarissa, 15, 28, 45
clinics, 44, 47–49

D

dating agency, 18, 32
Denis, 20, 29, 31–34, 36, 41, 47–48
doctors, 10, 42
Dr. Weinberg, 43–46

E

employment counselors, 15
exchange program, 7

F

father, 6, 27, 33–34
fibromas, 1, 9–10, 16, 41–46
    dermal, 10
    large, 42
Forum, 11
France, 16–17
French, 6–8, 32
French literature, 6

G

Germany, 7
Guinness, 27, 41

H

Hay, Louise, 13, 22–23, 39
healing therapy, 21, 45
high school, 6, 8–9
home, 8, 20, 36, 41

J

Jill, 49
job, 7–8, 11, 13, 15, 32

L

languages, 7–9

M

manicure, 13–14
Manon, 26
Marla, 42–43
Marshall, 27, 41

meditations, 22–23, 39
Mexico, 7–8
mother, 3, 5–6, 10–12, 16–17, 20, 34–35, 42–46, 53

N

Nadine, 26
nature-lover singles group, 31
neurofibromatosis, 1, 9–11, 13, 15–17, 19–23, 39, 42–44, 48, 52–53
Neurofibromatosis Society of Ontario Annual General Meeting, 52
NF1, 1–3

O

Oakville & Milton Humane Society, 41

P

pain, 9–10, 12, 17–18, 20, 22, 39, 44
parents, 2–3, 5–6, 8–10, 32, 35
pharmacy, 35–36
Port Credit, 26, 38, 41, 47
public school experiences, 6

R

Running Room, 47–49

S

salon, 13–14, 19–20
school, 3, 5–6, 8–9

Scotiabank Waterfront event, 48
Single Gourmet, 32
sisters, 7, 9, 34, 43
skin, 2, 10, 12–13, 19, 36
skin bumps, 11
skin condition, 13, 36, 52
soul mate, 31–32
spa director, 19
Spanish, 6
spa owner, 20
surgery, 10, 19, 41, 43–46
Switzerland, 6, 8

T

Toronto, 8, 32, 38
tumors, 1, 10, 43

ABOUT THE AUTHOR

Nicole Porlier (née Bolliger) was born in Toronto on October 2, 1966. Nicole's mother, Arlette Bolliger (née Deneffe), was born in Brussels, Belgium, and Nicole's father, Heinz Bolliger, was born in Gais, Appenzell, Switzerland.

Nicole has two older sisters, Nadine and Manon, who live with their spouses in Vancouver. She also has two nieces, Janael and Leana, as well as a nephew, Sagan.

Nicole graduated high school at North Toronto Collegiate Institute in 1985.

Although Nicole does not have a formal postsecondary diploma or certificate, she has taken many continuing education courses over the years and has traveled extensively to study and work in places such as Geneva and Mexico.

In her thirties, she found a job at a company called Ingram Micro, located in Mississauga.

In 2005, she lost her job at Ingram Micro due to restructuring and outsourcing. That same year, Denis and Nicole decided to open their own independent business called the Glass Half Full in Oakville, Ontario, which is a "ferment on premise" store. Denis and Nicole help customers make wine in small batches of thirty bottles each with a minimal time commitment and the same quality of store-bought wine at half the cost. Over time, they added to their product line Mister Beer Bottle Brew, Keurig, K-Cup, and

Nespresso machines. They have been in business for eight years now and are working hard to grow and expand.

Today, Nicole feels stronger than ever and has the confidence to overcome anything she is faced with.

Nicole lives with her husband, Denis; their cat, Guinness; and their dog, Marshall, in Port Credit, Ontario.

CPSIA information can be obtained at www.ICGtesting.com
Printed in the USA
LVOW11*2003091214

418037LV00003B/7/P